—»52«—
WAYS TO
BUILD YOUR
SELF-ESTEEM
A N D
CONFIDENCE

52
WAYS TO
BUILD YOUR
SELF-ESTEEM
AND
CONFIDENCE

Catherine E. Rollins

THOMAS NELSON PUBLISHERS
Nashville

Published in Nashville, Tennessee, by Oliver-Nelson Books, a division of
Thomas Nelson, Inc., Publishers, and distributed in Canada by Lawson
Falle, Ltd., Cambridge, Ontario.

Printed in the United States of America.

Library of Congress Cataloging-in-Publication Data

Rollins, Catherine E., 1950–
        52 ways to build your self-esteem and confidence / Catherine E. Rollins.
        p.   cm.
     ISBN 0-8407-9615-3 (pbk.)
        1.   Self-esteem—Problems, exercises, etc.   2.   Self-confidence—
Problems, exercises, etc.   I. Title.   II. Title: Fifty-two ways to build your
self-esteem and confidence.
BF697.5.S46R65   1992
158′.1—dc20   92-14600
                                                                                    CIP

                   1   2   3   4   5   6   —   97   96   95   94   93   92

To
Fred and Jan
and
Les and Bobi
with thanksgiving for
your lives and love

★ Contents

★ Introduction

We aren't born with high self-esteem and confidence. We must acquire them. From someone, somewhere.

The ideal purveyors of self-esteem and confidence are our parents. They sometimes fail, however. Generally, their failure is through unintentional neglect, oversight, or rejection created in part by circumstances over which they have little or no control. They rarely intend to fail at providing us a good foundation of self-value or the life skills we need to face adulthood with confidence. In many cases, *their* parents failed to provide for them all that they needed, and they simply are passing along a lack of good parenting skills. Unfortunately, we are capable of understanding that far better as adults than as children.

As children we only feel intuitively that our parents aren't giving us all that we need and that we are falling short of their full approval. We don't know that areas of the inner spirit are being dwarfed or untapped. We only know that we have

an ache for something more. Hurts take root. Inner wounds fester. And we emerge as adults who
are still hurt and wounded, now knowing a little
more clearly our deficiencies and sensing a little
more acutely our incompleteness, shortcomings,
and inadequacies.

What can we do? First, we must forgive our parents. Failing to forgive them only keeps us riding
the emotional merry-go-rounds of the past. Forgiveness frees us from their influence and allows
us to face adulthood squarely.

Second, we must face our hurts and our inadequacies—defining them the best we can and determining the best ways in which we can heal ourselves or put ourselves into a position where
others can assist us in the healing process.

Third, we must make a conscious decision to
move toward wholeness. We must decide within
ourselves that we *will* become whole adults. The
decision to build self-esteem and confidence is ultimately a definitive move toward becoming a more
complete person, whole in spirit, mind, emotions,
body, and relationships.

Some individuals are the products of bona fide
child abuse—physical, sexual, emotional, spiritual.
In these cases the pain inflicted is intentional, or at
least conscious, on the part of the perpetrator and
far more damaging to the victim. Forgiveness may
be harder to grant. The wounds may take longer to

heal. But the process of healing *is* possible. Nobody, no matter how difficult the early years, needs to remain shackled forever by a deficient self-concept or a lack of personal confidence.

Finally, a vast number of persons experienced wonderful childhoods only to suffer abuse as adults from other adults—perhaps spouses, supervisors, teachers, or even "friends." The abuse may come in the form of rejection. In these cases of adult-onset abuse, the person's otherwise healthy self-esteem and confidence suffer a severe whack, generally from the blind side. What was once believed with full assurance is suddenly shaken; what was once taken for granted is suddenly found to be shifting; what was once regarded as truth is suddenly suspect; what was once counted on is suddenly questioned.

Again, the process of growth is essentially the same: forgiving the hurtful party, facing one's wounds, and making a determined effort to become whole again.

This book is divided into two sections:

(1) a set of "foundational choices" that are basic to becoming whole or to regaining wholeness;
(2) a set of "practical action steps"—things to do to fill in the gaps of one's life, to repair the breaches, to heal the wounds.

Foundational Choices

1 ★ Choose Truth

Many of us would like to live forever in fantasy-lands of our own creation—sweeping evidence of reality under every magic carpet we can find. The concept we develop of ourselves in fantasyland, however, is inevitably *not* a true one.

To gain or regain a healthy self-identity, you must first choose to face the truth about yourself and then decide what to do about it.

Ask yourself these two key questions:

1. Can I recognize a lie when I hear one? Very often we aren't aware, or refuse to face the fact, that what we are being told simply isn't true—about events, about relationships and, most important, about ourselves. Often, we let proclamations of "love" cloud the truth. *"He said he loved me, so I believed that what he told me about myself was true." "She lied to me all the time, but it was too painful to face the fact that someone who loved me would lie to me."*

2. Do I tune out the truth or deny it?   If the answer is yes, ask yourself why. Why would you choose a lie over truth? Do you perceive truth as more painful than lies? In the long run, the lie always brings the greater pain. When you face the truth squarely with an optimistic attitude that "if it's wrong I can fix it, if it's sin I can repent of it, if it's bad I can seek a way to get to good," the truth is not only liberating but the first step toward a better tomorrow.

Several other questions related to truth are important to consider:

- Who is telling me who I am, what I can do, and defining my status and worth in life?

To whom are you giving the power for your definition? Is it a mother who died twenty years ago? A spouse? An adult child? You are the product of a series of definitions about yourself that you have accepted as being true. It helps to go back periodically and reevaluate to whom you have given this "power of definition."

- Are the people from whom I am deriving definitions of myself trustworthy?

What is their motivation for telling you things about yourself? What do they get out of it? Could they be wrong? Could they be misinformed? Could they be lying purposefully? Could they be inadvertently tearing you down to build themselves up? Could they be projecting on you their own feelings of inadequacy?

- Is the information I am taking into my being and adopting as true actually rooted in reality?

Can you cite evidence that supports the conclusions being drawn about yourself? Are you taking things at face value without substantiating them? Are you cross-examining the witnesses to your life?

In seeking the truth, choose to associate with those who tell the truth. Ask why persons believe what they say about you. Ask upon what evidence they base their conclusions. Question their motives.

And above all . . . if the "truth" they proclaim about you is all bad, demand that they also tell you the "truth" about you that is good. Only then can you even begin to achieve a balanced report. Be highly suspicious of the people who point out only your flaws and failures and never applaud your strengths and successes. They aren't telling you the whole story. And a partial story isn't truth.

2 ★ Choose Joy

Joy is a choice. Most people don't think so, but it is. We can choose to rejoice in life, or we can choose to be morose.

Sadness is a valid emotion. Sorrow is a part of the human experience. The continuum of emotions available to all of us includes the negative. There's a dark side to each one of us. In choosing joy, we are not negating the existence or the value of pain. We are simply choosing not to dwell there emotionally.

More Than Happiness Joy is more than happiness. Happiness is contingent on outer circumstances—the arrival of a happy surprise, the dawn of a bright morning, the cozy fireplace feeling of being curled up in the warmth of family love. Joy is rooted not in the external but in the internal. It's an attitude based on these beliefs:

- Life is important.
- Life has direction.
- Life has meaning and purpose.

- Life holds potential.
- Direction, meaning, and potential are all worth seeking and achieving.

Joy is rooted in the belief that life is *good* and that you are *good* and that both have the capacity for being better.

More Than Positive Thinking   Joy is more than positive thinking. It's more than getting up and saying repeatedly to the mirror, "I'm the greatest." Joy isn't "worked up"; it's brought forth. Joy is the spark at the core of your being that you *refuse* to allow to be extinguished, no matter how fierce the winds of woe are blowing or how dark the circumstances.

How can you increase your joy level today? Joy comes when you stare down fear and say, "I will not let fear swamp my boat. I will not let darkness overtake me. I will not let failure consume me. I will praise God and exult in life—no matter what."

Choose joy today. Choose to perceive yourself as a joyful person. You have the power to be that—no matter what other difficulties may lie ahead in your growth toward confidence and high self-esteem.

3 ★ Choose to Live

The person who has experienced a severe loss nearly always goes through at least one period in which he wishes he could crawl in a hole somewhere and pull it in over his head. Sometimes the wish becomes a strong desire to escape, withdraw, or just plain disappear for a while.

The emotional wounds that come with a loss are very real and very painful. We should never discount their impact or their potential to fester and turn into a malignant bitterness over time. The reaction of desiring to flee when wounded is a normal one. When the self has been injured in any way, the desire to withdraw from life is to be expected.

The critical moment comes, however, when you must choose to live again. Choose to reemerge. Choose to reembrace life. Choose to go on!

Choose a Rich, Full, Wonderful Life

Don't simply choose to survive. Try to look beyond the pain of the moment and envision a life in which you are *not* hanging on by your fingernails or just scraping by. Envision a future day in which you are once again strong, prosperous, and emotionally vibrant.

Choose a Life That Has Meaning and Purpose Establish a reason in your own heart and mind to go forward in life. You may need to talk to a professional counselor in helping to determine what *you* still see as a "purpose" or use for your life.

Each person has something to give. Including *you!* What can you still contribute to others? Think about it. Write it down. Then . . . choose to give it. In so doing, you'll be choosing to live and not die.

4 ★ Choose Today

Every morning offers you a new opportunity to start over—to enjoy a success, to be all that you can be, to live life to the fullest.

The tendency when faced with a severe blow to esteem or confidence is to dwell on what once was.

Closing the Door on the Past The person who is down on himself nearly always blames himself for the failures of the past. It's helpful to sort out the past in order to

- determine what part of the failure was truly yours.
- analyze what you did that contributed to the failure—the decisions you made, the actions you took, the timing of your actions, the faulty rationale or incorrect evidence upon which you acted, and so forth.
- resolve what it is that you should have done, which, in effect, is a resolution about what you would do if faced with a similar set of circumstances in the future.

Forgive yourself for your part of the failure, make whatever amends and recompenses you can make or you believe should be made, and then close the door on the past. Choose *not* to dwell there. Choose not to live your life looking in the rearview mirror.

Keeping the Future at Arm's Length   A second tendency of the person with low self-esteem is to look at the future and say, "I don't have what it takes to be successful again (or ever)." The key question to ask yourself is this: Why not? What has changed about *you*—not what has changed about the circumstances around you? You may have been deeply wounded, rejected, or abused, but the core of the inner you—your talents, personality traits, experiences, acquired skills, inherent creativity—can never be stolen or destroyed by another person. That part of you can only be sealed over by you. You do *have* what it takes to forge a wonderful future.

- Learn to live a *successful* day. Include in your daily plan the acquisition of one or two daily habits that you consider to be good.

Set one or two goals of "things to do" for yourself personally. Focus on a goal or two for the workday. Take stock as the day closes and contemplate for a few moments what you did right during the day.

- If you find that you are not successful in reaching your daily goals, readjust them so that you will be!

You may be biting off more than you can chew. Your successful day may include nothing more than the fact that you got dressed, ate three meals, walked the dog, took out the trash, made two phone calls, and went to the grocery store. Success is what *you* define it to be.

What happens when you string together a series of mostly successful days? You end up with a successful life. Choose to live today. It's the only time you truly can control.

5 ★ Choose to Grow

Do you remember how you felt as a child in the presence of grown-ups? Grown-ups had it easy. They could do what they wanted when they wanted, and they could call the shots.

But if anything, life seems to get harder with time. Adults certainly don't get to call all the shots they'd like to call. You come to realize, however, that it's good always to be growing.

Growing means changing. And change is scary. It requires a risk. Choose to take it. Every person I've ever known who undertook a growth change said as he or she emerged on the other side, "I'm glad I did that. It was worth it. I'm better off today than I was then."

Get Professional Counsel You may find great opportunities for growth by talking with an expert in the area in which you desire to grow. If you need career advice, talk to a career counselor. If you need psychological help, talk to a psychologist. If you need spiritual help, seek out a minister or priest who is trained in counseling.

Gain New Information To keep growing mentally, you need a steady dose of "input." Information comes in a wide variety of packages: courses, manuals, magazines, movies, galleries, museums, libraries. Avail yourself of the best teachers you can find.

Gather New Experiences Ever been on a roller coaster? Ever seen the ocean? Ever climbed a mountain?

A part of the growing process in a relationship—personal or professional—invariably seems to require confrontation. Learn to fight fairly with those around you. Learn ways in which to explore and communicate and set goals. Getting past the confrontation may involve a mutual decision to pursue counseling, gain information, or gather experience . . . together.

There's really no such thing as "just maintaining forever." Maintaining is possible for a while, and the person who suffers a blow to his self-esteem sometimes needs to "just maintain." (Often, that's all he can do. In those cases, maintaining a regimen of sleeping, eating, working, playing is actually growth—it's building up strength.) Eventually, we all need to move beyond what seems to be a "just maintaining" state. In the long run of life, what isn't growing is starting to die.

Choose growth. It's a part of choosing life.

6 ★ Choose to Forgive

"Forgive and forget" is a phrase known to all of us. It's bad advice, however, because it's not possible for any of us ever to forgive and forget.

Forgiveness is possible. Forgetting isn't.

No matter how hard you may try, you can never truly forget an experience you've had. Brain researchers tell us that any person with a normal brain can be made to recall *any* incident that has occurred in his or her life. You do not carry all of the information you have in your conscious mind, but you never lose any information once you have acquired it. It's always lurking within someplace.

The good news is that forgiveness brings a sense of order, resolution, and meaning to all of the events of our past that we cannot forget. In that, forgiveness heals.

Not the Prosecutor It takes tremendous emotional and mental energy to be another person's prosecutor. You constantly must appraise what she did in the light of current consequences. You must think about her continually to try to understand her motives for the crime. You must always be looking for evidence related to her behavior. Actually, it's emotionally exhausting to stand as prosecutor for another person.

Not the Judge   It also takes wisdom that none of us has to be another person's judge. You can never fully understand another person—know all of his reasons for doing and saying certain things, know everything about his background or personality, or know with certainty that your "sentence" for him is the most just or redemptive one.

The forgiving person says,

- "I think you were a lousy parent. But I no longer hold that against you. I take the responsibility for my adulthood on myself. I forgive you for what you did, and I release you from having an ongoing influence in my life today."
- "I think you were an abusive spouse. But I no longer want to dwell on your abuse. I mentally and emotionally am letting you go so that I can be free."
- "I think you were wrong to fire me. But I refuse to focus my thoughts on you any longer. I release you from my mind and my heart. I choose instead to look forward to my next job."
- "I don't believe you really tried to help me or

to assist my growth. But I choose to forgive you for not being all that I think you should have been for me. I choose to be responsible for my own life, to get the assistance I need, and to make the growth I desire."

Forgiveness frees you to deal with your present and make plans for your future. It puts you into a position where you are no longer "under the influence" of another person's critical behavior—including the behavior that damages your self-esteem and injures your confidence.

7 ★ Choose to Receive

You didn't acquire unhealthy self-esteem on your own. Somebody helped you along in the process of your thinking poorly about yourself. Through critical comments, negative put-downs, or lack of attention or positive feedback, the person (or persons) assisted in your lack of self-development.

The converse is also true. You won't acquire healthy self-esteem entirely on your own.

Choose to be around people who have healthy self-esteem Talk to them and watch them. Learn from them. Ask their advice.

Choose to be around people who will build you up Everybody needs a cheerleader. That doesn't mean the other person is blind to your faults or impervious to your bad behavior—only that the person *wants* to see you succeed and grow and is willing to cheer you on.

Choose to associate with people who are growing Their enthusiasm for life will inspire you. The insights they draw from their own growth will help you.

Choose to align yourself with people who truly want to be your friend and whom you want to befriend in return There are millions of positive, encouraging, growing people in the world. You can't have all of them as friends. Seek to develop a few close friendships in which you are both generous giver and generous receiver.

Choose to associate with people who have a giving attitude toward the world Associate with people who want to make a contribution to life, who want to see problems solved, needs met, improvements made, bad situations resolved. Don't expect to be the object of their giving as much as a cogiver with them.

Choose to receive the good things that people desire to give you Don't shun their constructive help. Don't disregard their compliments. Don't turn them away when they offer to be with you in a difficult moment. Open up and receive what they have for you.

The person with low self-esteem is often wary. Too many people have hurt her in the guise of trying to help. He has been wounded in the name of love. If that's the case in your life, you'll need to make a conscious choice to open up and receive.

- Choose your givers wisely.
- Choose to receive only what helps you.
- Choose to receive only what you can contain.

The more good, positive, upbuilding information and opinions you receive into yourself about yourself, the more your self-esteem will grow.

Practical Action
Steps

8 ★ Just Say No

Is someone telling you . . .
"You're not good enough,"
"You aren't acceptable,"
"You don't have what it takes,"
"You're unlovable,"
"You're not worth it"?
Just say, "No. You're wrong about me."

Stand your ground! Don't lie down and let another person trample over your soul.

Before you adopt a strong defensive position, make certain you understand fully the statement being made about you. With as much control and quiet resolve as you can muster, question the person until you get to the real intent of the statement:

- "Are you saying that I don't have what it takes because I lack certain skills or training, or is it because you think I'm defective as a person?"
- "Are you saying that I'm unlovable because you lack the capacity to love me, or are there certain attributes or behaviors that you don't

like?" (Always assume that like and love are two different emotions, and that they don't always accompany each other.)

- "On what evidence are you concluding that I'm unacceptable? Is it my qualifications or my personhood that makes me unacceptable?"

It's Your Right   It's your right to have an answer to accusations against your personhood. The answers may not be what you want to hear, but listen very closely to them to learn all that you need to learn. If, indeed, you lack specific skills and attributes, take the position that those are things you can learn or develop. The reason you are being rejected has to do with qualifications, not the quality of your personhood.

If, on the other hand, the statement is against who you are—calling into question your right to exist, your basic human rights, or your legal rights —stand firm and challenge the remark. Say, "I disagree with you. I think you have an erroneous (or limited) perception of me." State your reasons for drawing that conclusion.

"But what if the person is bigger than I am?" you may ask. (Which may also be stated as "stronger than I am," "more powerful than I am," or "smarter than I am.") Stand your ground anyway.

You Deserve Better Even if someone attempts to use force against you, declare, "You have no right to do this to me or to say this to me. I deserve better."

You may need to appeal to a higher authority if you feel you are being accused unjustly.

You may need to seek legal action.

You may need to get away. (There's little point in standing your ground to the point of being murdered or maimed.)

In so doing, however, make sure you are taking an action that you choose. Even if you shout it to the wind . . . or whisper it to your mirror . . . make a proclamation within yourself, "I am valuable. I am worthy to be loved. I may make mistakes, but I am a person of worth."

Say no to the person who attempts to put you down or chip away at your self-worth. Say no to the person who attempts to undermine your self-confidence. In so doing, you are saying yes to yourself.

9 ★ Don't Belittle Yourself

You've probably heard someone say,
"Oh, I don't deserve this."
Or "I'm just a nobody."
Or "That's out of my league."
Are you guilty of making statements like that about yourself?
Are you guilty of calling yourself stupid or any other of a vast number of derogatory terms?
If so . . . stop it.

Never, Never, Never Belittle Yourself

We each have enough trouble withstanding the jealous, unwise, careless, hurtful remarks of others. We don't need to heap even more coals on our own heads.

What happens when you make a negative remark about yourself?

- First, you reinforce that very idea in your own mind.

Your own two ears are usually the closest ears to your own mouth. If you believe yourself, you begin to think of yourself as you describe yourself!

- Second, you plant the idea in the minds of others.

Soon, they'll be saying to themselves, "Well, if she thinks she's stupid, she probably is," or "If he thinks he's a fool, chances are that he knows what he's talking about." Others begin to think of you exactly as you ask them to think of you, and the next thing you know, they'll be treating you according to the way you've suggested they treat you —as if you're a fool, a klutz, or a loser!

If you claim to another person that you don't deserve something . . . next time you probably won't receive it. If you tell another person that you're worthless . . . the next time you come up for a raise, you probably won't get it. If you claim to be a nobody . . . next time you probably won't be invited to go along.

Play It Straight   "But," you may protest, "I'm just teasing."

Don't do it. When it comes to who you are, play it straight.

"But," you say, "if I don't say something like that, people will think I'm proud."

You don't need to say something prideful. Rather

than say something derogatory about yourself, don't say anything at all! Or just say, "Thank you" or "Wow" or "What a country!" or "I have it on the highest authority that I'll do better next time!"

You can be surprised that you won the award, but don't say, "Oh, you should have chosen someone else."

You can be thankful that you received the honor, but don't say, "Wow, I really don't deserve this."

You can be intrigued by why someone asked you to come along or be a part or take the new role, but don't say, "Are you sure you chose the right person?"

People tend to think of you as you tell them to think. Therefore, tell them well.

10 ★ Stare Down Your Greatest Fear

Fear is the silent companion of low self-esteem. People who struggle with low self-esteem usually express a deep feeling of fear. In many cases, that feeling of fear is referred to as a rather "uneasy feeling," a "worry," or a feeling of being "troubled." When questioned about it, the person often doesn't know what is bothering him, or he may be able to describe uneasy situations without being able to label the fear.

The fear is ultimately one common to all of us: the fear of being alone. Scientists have told us for decades that all babies are born with two fears: the fear of falling, and the fear of sudden noises. Both fears are closely associated with birth: the quiet, muffled noises of the womb are suddenly disrupted as the baby "falls" from its mother's womb into a completely new and much noisier environment. What a traumatic experience that would be for us adults if we found ourselves in a similar situation, even if we knew the outcome would be tolerable!

Separation is also a part of the birthing process.

With the cutting of the umbilical cord we are no longer vitally connected to another human being in what had seemed to us to be an inseparable relationship. In many ways, we all long for that closeness, intimacy, and feeling of being "one" with another throughout our lives. The fear of losing connection seems to be a basic fear rooted in the emotions, just as fears of falling and loud noises are rooted in physical instincts.

Are you fearful today? Do you feel as if something is bothering you deep down inside your spirit?

Face that fear. Name it. Confront it.

Admit It to Yourself   "I'm afraid of being alone. I don't want to be alone. I don't like the idea of being alone."

Face Up to the Fact   "I am alone. I've been alone for years, and I've survived. Even though I may have wonderful relationships with others, I will ultimately be alone. Even in the best marriage, the most loving family environment, the most meaningful work relationship . . . I am an individual who is responsible for my own actions, ideas, choices, and responsibilities. That's life. And I can make the most of it."

Recognize It "Every other person on the planet is also afraid of being alone. Nobody wants to be alone any more than I do. If I am rejected or disconnected from one person, there are literally hundreds of thousands of other people with whom I might establish a connection."

Be Hopeful "Since we are all longing for a connection, I will do my best to reach out to others who are just as fearful of being alone as I am. I will not expect them to do more for me than they can do; I will do all I can do to be a loyal friend (spouse, family member, colleague) to them."

Fear cripples us from being ourselves and from exercising our talents and pursuing our potential.

When, out of fear, you don't express yourself freely, you cut off a part of who you are and what you can be. You limit yourself. Low self-esteem and lack of confidence result because ultimately, in limiting your actions, you convince yourself that you can't do certain things or aren't capable of reaching certain goals.

Self-esteem begins to grow when you face your greatest fear and stare it down.

11 ★ Conduct a Personal Inventory

The person with low self-esteem rarely sees beyond her own nose. She is often far more preoccupied with herself than the person with high self-esteem. Growth occurs when a person is able to stand back and take an objective look at herself—to appraise herself as she would someone else.

If you have trouble doing this, ask someone to help you be objective about yourself. Choose someone you trust to tell you the truth—a trusted friend, a minister, or a professional counselor.

Put Your Inventory on Paper That way, you'll be able to refer to it later and be encouraged at seeing your growth over time. No personal inventory is ever final. It should constantly be in a state of positive change.

List Your Assets Fixed personal assets are those with which you were born—such as a strong physical constitution, family members you consider good role models, or musical ability. Note all of your personality strengths and talents. Liquid assets are those things you have acquired in life—training, education, experiences, associations, and friendships. (Sometimes friends and colleagues are the finest assets you have!)

Identify Your Goals Your goals and dreams are a part of who you are as a person. They are often the reason you act as you do. Generally speaking, the person with low self-esteem has lower and fewer goals than the person with high self-esteem. If you don't have any goals, take this opportunity to set some!

Identify Your Beliefs What do you feel strongly about? What are your spiritual values? What is your ethical code? Your value system is the "energy" behind your actions; it nearly always correlates with the intensity of your motivation. Very often, the person with low self-esteem loses sight of her beliefs, or her value system becomes weak. Writing down what you believe provides a good exercise in reappraising your inner spiritual life.

Identify Your Liabilities Take a moment to question what you listed as your liabilities. Ask yourself why you placed them in that category. You may be relating your liabilities to your goals—using them as excuses for why you can't succeed or aren't succeeding. That's rarely valid.

All of your "liabilities" are liquid. The more closely you look at them, the more likely you are to erase them from the list. Make that the final part of your personal inventory.

Identify Specific Actions to Turn Liabilities into Assets   What can you do by yourself? What requires assistance from others? Where can you get that assistance? Set a timetable for yourself to convert liabilities into assets. Some perceived liabilities may never become true "assets" to you, but they can at least become neutralized so that they really don't stand in the way of your achieving your goals or acting on your beliefs.

Now, stand back and take a look at the overall picture. If you are truly objective, you'll probably find that you have a great many more assets— counting your dreams, beliefs, goals, and friends as assets—than you have liabilities. Your liabilities generally can be converted to assets or at least become neutral factors in your life.

Take stock of who you *really* are!

12 ★ Map Out a Plan

After you have completed your personal inventory, take a second related step and map out a personal growth plan.

Review Your Assets What can you do to strengthen them? How can you enrich your friendships and professional associations? What can you do to gain more information or acquire more skills in your area of interest or expertise?

Review Your Goals Are they realistic? Are they really ones you want to *work* to achieve? Eliminate the goals that are just wishful thinking or idle daydreaming. Eliminate all goals based on random chance. (Winning the state lottery is *not* an acceptable goal—it's a fanciful wish!) Break your goals into subgoals or components. Identify a series of small steps you can take to get to your final destination.

How do some of your goals interrelate? Are there any areas in which you may be able to reach two goals with one activity?

Review Your Beliefs How can you act on them? What specific things can you do to test, reinforce, or activate the things you hold as important values?

Doing and Being Make lists. Set timetables. Focus on a regimen that will help you make your days, weeks, and months count toward the accomplishment of the goals important to you.

"All this doing," you may moan. "When do I get to the being—the relaxing moments, the taking of life as it comes?"

Lists don't preclude spontaneity. In many cases, they allow for it! Schedules don't preclude quiet times, recreation, or periods of "soaking" in beauty and rest. They can accommodate downtime.

For most people, doing and being are so tightly interrelated they really can't be separated. We are what we do; we act based on who we are. Even the most peaceful, laid-back person *does* certain things that create that feeling within his being.

The real issue is one of intentionality. Do you want to have healthier self-esteem? Then you probably need to focus your life more. Do you want more confidence? Then there's a necessary doing of certain things to achieve it.

13 ★ Stop Comparing

The person with low self-esteem and confidence nearly always has developed the bad habit of comparing himself or herself to others.

- "I'm just not as pretty as Susie."
- "I'm not as smart as Gerald."
- "I didn't come from the same privileged background as Margaret."
- "I didn't have the same opportunity for education as Barrett."

Stop comparing. You're engaging in a lie.

A lie? Yes! Comparisons are usually based on inaccurate information and are thus false to some degree.

In the First Place You don't know all there is to know about that other person. You don't really know Gerald's IQ or his aptitude scores in various areas of learning. You don't really know all the details of Margaret's background or the inside story on the financial aid package that made Barrett's education possible. Every person has something to overcome to achieve success in life. Every "win" has its price in terms of time, effort, and resources.

In the Second Place   Comparisons are often used as excuses for failure: *"I didn't get the job (or the promotion, the raise, the date, the award, the honor) . . . because . . . I'm not as smart as Gerald (as pretty as Susie, and so forth)."* Again, that's probably not the case.

By using an excuse, you are lying to yourself. You aren't facing up to the real reasons behind what you perceive to be a loss. You aren't acknowledging the fact that you were popping gum during the interview, your appearance was sloppy, you used bad grammar (which you need to relearn), you didn't fill out the application completely, you ridiculed the other person, you don't have the proper qualifications, or any of an infinite number of other reasons.

In gaining self-esteem and confidence, you must first tell the truth about yourself and limit your concern to yourself. You must take the blame for your failures to be able to applaud your successes.

14 ★ Stand Tall

This observation holds true regardless of age, sex, race, physical stature, or beauty:

The person with high self-esteem stands up straight, sits tall, and walks with boldness. The person with low self-esteem slouches, slinks, bows his head down, curls his shoulders forward, and frequently sits in knots.

No matter how much makeup the person may have on, the precision of the hairstyle, the gleam on the boots, or the cost of the clothing . . . regardless of any of the jewelry or related accessories (including the model of car) . . . a person who stands tall, sits tall, and walks tall considers herself to be a woman of value and inner strength, a woman with the potential for success.

The minute you make the decision within yourself to grow in self-esteem and confidence, make a second decision: I'm going to "move tall" this day forward.

Shoulders back and head up.

A bold stride—even if you are just walking from one room to the next in your own home.

A square-to-the-world attitude!

Physical Well-Being When you take on a new posture, you'll feel better physically. Good posture is linked in many ways to overall health.

Psychological Well-Being You'll feel better psychologically. Not all signals in your being come from the brain first; in the case of posture, your body is also sending a signal to your brain. If you walk tall, you'll soon be thinking tall. Reach for the sky with your head, and you tend to reach for the sky with your attitude.

When you communicate a message of strength, authority, and self-value, others will treat you with more respect. You'll find that others are less likely to try to put you down. The more they treat you with respect, the more likely you are to feel positive about who you are.

Think "tall and straight" today!

15 ★ Smile

Nothing warms the heart, including your own heart, like a smile! Researchers are discovering more and more about the helpful chemicals released into the bloodstream as the result of laughter, smiles, and positive attitudes. The "merry heart" described by sages of old really "does good, like medicine."

Apart from the physical benefits of a smiling attitude lie the emotional ones. A person simply cannot laugh uproariously for a prolonged period without feeling a little bit better on the inside, too.

Smile at Yourself Learn to laugh at your foibles. The human condition is laughable in many ways; we all act the fool and perform the ridiculous at times—even the person who seems most poised and coolheaded. Don't laugh at yourself with ridicule; laugh at the fact that sometimes you do yourself in, generally in the craziest ways at the least opportune times. Turn loose and laugh *with* yourself, not *at* yourself.

Smile to Yourself Greet yourself in the morning with a grin. More important, call up memories that bring a smile to your face. That's one of the wonderful benefits of pleasurable experiences —you can recall them later for a second, even hundredth, moment of enjoyment.

Smile at Others Strangers. Friends. Co-workers. Your own family members. Spread the joy around. It's difficult to maintain a frown for very long in the presence of someone who is smiling!

Get back in touch with those things that once caused you to laugh with a hold-your-sides, belly-shaking laugh. Let go and have a little fun.

The person with low self-esteem tends to take life—and herself, or lack of self—far too seriously. Lighten up.

16 ★ Get Up and Get Out

The person with low self-esteem often hides from the world.

Set for yourself a minimal goal of achieving the "three *G*'s" every day.

Get Up   Get out of bed. Don't stay there. If you return to bed during the day for a nap, don't get back into your nightwear—lie down with your street clothes on.

By getting out of bed, you are exerting an attitude of "I choose to be well."

Of course, you can sleep in occasionally, you can retire early, or you can choose to spend an entire vacation day lounging around in your robe and pajamas. But as the norm of your life, choose to be out of bed, not in it.

Get Dressed   Shower (or bathe). Shave (if you do). Comb your hair. Get dressed. Put on your makeup (if you wear it). Face the day. You may not leave the neighborhood, but look as if you are ready to face the public.

Getting dressed helps you adopt the attitude that you are ready to do something or experience something—that you are expecting something to happen in your life and you're ready for it!

Get Out of the House   Even if you just walk around the block or sit outside on the porch, deck, or patio, get out of the four walls of your own space and give yourself the opportunity to interact with nature and with people. Both are God's gifts to you. Learn to see them as such and to avail yourself of the good things they have to offer you.

In all of your "getting" self-esteem . . . get up and get going!

17 ★ Have a Little Pep Talk with Yourself

Sometimes it helps to be your own cheerleader.

Give Voice to Your Good Opinions about Yourself Don't just "think" good about yourself; speak those good words aloud. You'll hear yourself, and the words will have a double opportunity to take root in your spirit. Say to yourself,

- "I can do this."
- "I'm worth it."
- "I'm able to learn this."
- "I'm going to try this."

People with low self-esteem get that way in part because they don't have someone else telling them how valuable and worthy they are. If you don't have someone else around to tell you how great you are, to applaud your bright moments, or to reinforce your good qualities—or if you missed out on having someone build you up in the past—tell yourself!

Readjust Your Memories   Go back in memory to times when you succeeded, performed well, or did a good job—especially those times when nobody seemed to notice or say anything to you—and compliment yourself. Say aloud, "You know, you really did a good job in making that model airplane," or "You sang every word of the song while lots of children around you were lip-synching," or "That was a great water color painting you did," or "I'm proud of you for getting a 90 on your history test."

Take a clue from the tennis courts. Players pump themselves up during a match. It works for them, and it will work for you!

18 ★ Adopt Healthy Habits

The person with low self-esteem frequently falls into a habit of not caring for herself. That often includes physical care as well as emotional care.

Adopt a healthy daily regimen.

Good Nutrition Fuel yourself with the freshest foods and the purest water. Avoid "junk" foods and foods high in salt, fat, and sugar.

Regular Meals Three squares a day and an optional snack—that's the routine followed by most health care facilities in the nation and the finest spas around the world! If it's good for them, it's a good policy for your home.

If you have difficulty cooking or you simply don't want to cook, you still have lots of options. Order in. Eat out. Hire a cook. These options may sound expensive, but many times they are less expensive than purchasing food that you end up throwing away.

Sufficient Sleep Eight or nine quality hours of sleep, uninterrupted, are considered the goal for most people (as supported by recent research). You may need to adopt an earlier lights-out policy at your house; you may need to adjust your schedule; you may need to quit working into the wee hours of the morning; you may need to make sleep a priority. Whatever it takes, get your Z's.

People Contact For at least a portion of your day, be with other people with whom you can spend relaxed moments and have unhurried conversation—to talk over the hurdles overcome or faced, your successes, the latest joke you heard, the funny thing that happened on the way home, the new products you saw in the store, the up-to-date news in the world, your community, your neighborhood, your life, your opinions.

Play Time Devote at least one part of each day to fun. If exercise is "work" to you, it doesn't count. Your fun activity may be a hobby, a game, a sport, a fix-it project, a movie, or a book. Do something that completely takes your mind off work and problems. If you work with your hands all day, your fun activity may be something that engages your mind. If you work with your mind all day, try doing something with your hands. TV doesn't count as play. While it may entertain, it doesn't replenish. Choose an activity about which you can say afterward, "That sure was fun. I had a great time." Indulge in laughter.

Centering Time   Set aside at least a few minutes of each day for quiet solitude. Learn to enjoy being alone. Use the time for reading inspirational literature . . . for praying . . . for just thinking. Focus on the larger issues of life, not personal problems. Daydream. Imagine. Think big thoughts.

A daily discipline with these components sends a signal to your psyche: you have balance; you have health. The healthy balanced person is a prime candidate for high self-esteem!

19 ★ Say No to Chemical Snares

Even as you say yes to health on a daily basis, say no to those things that would rob you of your health.

The person with low self-esteem sometimes turns to chemicals—including alcohol—as a means of bolstering confidence or improving self-perception.

In the long run, chemicals don't improve confidence or self-esteem; they help only to mask—temporarily—the lack of esteem and confidence.

Say no to chemicals you don't need for normal bodily function Assume that any chemicals you take are ones required by your particular body for restoring normal function. For example, an aspirin may help you get rid of a headache. Don't assume that you need two aspirin every four hours for the rest of your life to keep a headache from returning. On the other hand, if you are a diabetic who is insulin dependent, take that insulin. Your particular body needs it for normal function.

Don't assume that any medication you take is going to be necessary for a lifetime Some medications may be in this category, especially those for chronic heart patients. Other medications should be allowed to run their course, with no expectation of your refilling a prescription. Don't assume that because you are prescribed a tranquilizer or an antidepressant to get through a particularly difficult period you will always need the medication. Most drugs are prescribed for singular ailments that pass within a month!

Take prescription medicines only as they are prescribed Don't take more than one prescribed medication at a time without checking first with your physician. Always ask about side effects, especially those that might occur when two or more medications react with each other inside your body. Never assume that if one pill works well, two pills will work twice as well.

Never take a chemical to enhance your ability to do something Whether you want to relax, have more energy, be more creative, work longer hours, or improve muscle strength, such drugs will inevitably do you more harm than good.

Never take a chemical to enhance your perceived social status Participating in "chemical events" enhances your status only with others who are participating—in other words, your status is enhanced only by those who are already addicted, misinformed, misled, rebellious, or unwise. Associating with those folks is detrimental to your self-esteem.

If you find that you are becoming addicted to a prescribed medication, talk to your doctor about safe ways to get off the drug   Don't attempt to go "cold turkey" or to detox yourself.

Face up to the fact that alcohol and nicotine are drugs   Don't get started on these substances. If you're already addicted, get help to free yourself. You'll feel better physically, and you'll have a great sense of victory in overcoming the addiction.

Chemically induced feelings of self-esteem are always a poor substitute for the real thing.

20 ★ Associate with High-Esteem People

Choose to be around people who are confident and have a balanced, healthy perspective about themselves. Choose to associate with individuals who value themselves and others. Choose to participate in activities and projects with men and women who are growing—who are setting high goals for themselves and are on the path toward achieving them.

You'll Be Inspired You'll find that the hours spent in the presence of high-esteem people pass quickly and productively. You'll feel encouraged to try new things, and you'll gain a desire to do more and be more.

You'll Be Helped People with high self-esteem are nearly always givers. They are frequently teachers or mentors at heart—people who desire to help others reach their full potential, even as they seek to reach their own. Accept their help and advice.

You'll Be Instructed   You'll learn by watching them—not only in the area of work skills but in the areas of communication and interpersonal skills. Be open to their suggestions.

Want to learn something? Find the person most confident in his knowledge of it or his ability in it!

In a famous art gallery one afternoon, a dozen or so art students were copying the great paintings before them. Their teacher said of this practice: "You must copy in order to learn technique, to get a foundation. Later, you can choose your own subjects and your own style." Good advice!

The more you associate with high-esteem people and the more you emulate their behaviors and mind-set, the more you'll esteem yourself, and the more others will regard you with greater respect.

21 ★ Treat Yourself

Indulge yourself occasionally. Just because.

- It might be taking a long relaxing bubble bath.
- It might be ordering a favorite food in a favorite restaurant.
- It might be exploring the shops in a certain area for an entire afternoon.
- It might be going to the movies all by yourself.

Whatever your choice of a treat, give yourself a dose of pleasure.

Inexpensive Indulgences   You may need to hire a baby-sitter to indulge yourself. Do so! You need to feel good about yourself if you are ever going to transmit a good feeling to your child.

You need not, however, spend a great deal of money on your indulgence. The indulgence may be time alone. A walk in the park at noon may suffice, at no cost (and with the added benefit of exercise).

Occasional Indulgences   You shouldn't make a habit of your indulgence. Otherwise, it will soon cease to be a treat. A chocolate sundae every afternoon isn't an indulgence; it's overkill.

Choose an occasional indulgence that represents something you might not otherwise do or that you might expect someone else to do for you.

Buy yourself a bouquet of flowers. Enjoy them!

Give yourself an occasional gift.

About once a year, one fellow takes a roll of quarters and goes down to the local video arcade to play all of the games. "For two hours, I'm a carefree, spendthrift teenager again," he says. "The rest of the year I can be grown up."

You treat people you like. You gift people you respect or wish to honor. The acts are no less important when you are the recipient.

22 ★ Point Out the Positive

When someone calls attention to the negative about a situation or speaks a word of negative criticism, choose to speak up for the positive—especially if the negative comment is about you!

"I'm Me" What do you say when someone says to you, "You're not as good a cook as Sally," or "You're not as good an *anything* as someone else"? Respond, "Perhaps not. I agree with you that Sally is a good cook. But I'm probably a lot better than Sally at other things. I'm me. Sally's Sally. Each of us has different strengths and weaknesses. Let me remind you about one of my strengths."

"See My Good Points" What do you say when someone says to you, "You're a slob"? First, ask for a definition of the term. What is it that the person doesn't like? Insist on concrete statements. Don't deny the fact that you may be "part slob"; at the same time, don't take on a total identity of a slob! Respond, "There's some merit in what you say, and I'll work on it. But there's also a good side to me. Everybody has some good and bad points. I hope you can see my good points, too."

"What Do You Like?"   What do you say when someone says to you, "I don't like the way you do your hair"? Respond, "Thank you for expressing your opinion. What do you like about me today?"

"I Have Strengths"   Always bring a negative-commenting person back to the positive. Insist on being considered as a whole person with both bad and good qualities—flaws you are working on and strengths you are seeking to enhance.

At times, you may need to insist that the person admit the flaw is a small one, not one of cosmic proportions or importance. Few flaws are fatal, either to you or to others. You can respond, "Yes, I do have that fault. I'm working on it. I'm sorry it irritates you. But I also know that this isn't something of life-or-death consequences."

The person with low self-esteem frequently tunes in only to negative comments. He frequently fails to stand up for his own positive attributes. Insist that others speak positive things to you each time they speak negatives.

23 ★ Make Something with Your Hands

Create something with your own two hands. It might be something for utility or beauty or fun:

- Something you make out of wood—a piece of furniture, a frame, a doghouse, a birdfeeder, a deck, or a candlestick
- Something you paint or draw
- Something you sew by machine or hand
- Something you create in ceramic or clay—a piece of sculpture or something you spin out on a potter's wheel
- Something you put together—a model, a dollhouse for your little girl, or a swing set for the backyard

Achievement How does working with your hands relate to self-esteem? Projects made by hand have an obvious beginning, middle, and ending. When you're finished with the day's work, you can see your progress. When you're finished with the project, you can rejoice in your achievement. A finished handcraft says to you and to others, "I am a person capable of making things."

Skill   A project made by hand calls for skill. Your work may be crude because your skills aren't perfectly honed. That's OK. Consider it one of your "earlier works." The handmade object says to you and to others, "I have a skill. I'm still developing it, but the good news is that I'm growing in this ability. I'm capable of learning."

Planning   Made-by-hand projects require some planning and nearly always an ability to read and follow instructions. The finished product says, "I can think, and I can translate what I read into something I can do. I am an intelligent person!"

The handmade object is a reflection of you— your intelligence, your artistry and craftsmanship, your ability to make choices in life, your time and, above all, your ability to set a goal and discipline yourself to reach it, piece by piece or step by step.

24 ★ Grow a Garden

Gardens represent life . . . beauty . . . health . . . nourishment. They reflect the seasons. They put you in touch with the great rhythms of life, growth, and death. Grow one! It will help you grow in esteem.

Flowers or vegetables, the choice is yours. Do all the work or only part of it. Do, however, make certain that you occasionally put your hands into the soil and touch the plants. Don't just watch your garden as a process from afar. Take an active part in its design, development, and cultivation.

Working in the earth and with plants does several things to build your self-esteem:

A garden puts you in touch with the Creator That is almost always a sure reminder of your status as a unique created being. Notice how each plant is different, how each flower has a slightly different character. Notice how different colors and textures blend together. Isn't the variety in your garden incredible? Reflect on your individuality and the ways in which you are distinctly different from, and yet capable of blending with, those around you.

A garden reminds you of the value of all living things
Everything within the natural world has a function and purpose. Human beings function in similar ways. Each of us has something within that is capable of nourishing others. You have beauty to give. You have talents that can blend with those of others and messages that are important to communicate to others.

A garden reminds you of many natural law and spiritual law principles You are confronted with the principle of a seed. Although you may plant it and water it, a power far greater than that of a human being actually causes the seed to grow. You are confronted with the fact of weeds and insect pests. Your life, too, is often plagued by unwanted intrusions. A garden encourages you that you can survive transplanting, pruning, and hard freezes.

A garden reminds you of your role as a steward of the earth You are a caretaker of the world around you.

A garden reminds you that nothing flourishes without nourishment and care Just as garden plants need water, sunlight, fertilizer, and daily care, so you must avail yourself of the nourishment you need.

A garden reminds you of the joys of the process
There's great pleasure in the planting and cultivating stages of life, not only the harvest.

25 ★ Don't Do It All

The person with low self-esteem often fails to delegate responsibilities or chores to others. He becomes so accustomed to thinking of himself as the "doer" that he willingly takes on all the less-than-elegant work of life without questioning whether it is truly his obligation or job.

This is not to say that any work is beneath the dignity of any person. All work has value, and all jobs have merit. It is to say that always being at the whim and command of others to do tasks outside one's job description is not characteristic of a person of healthy self-esteem. The person with healthy self-esteem is always willing to do whatever it legitimately takes to grow and achieve, but she isn't willing to be "used" by others.

Learn to Delegate (and to Delegate Fairly) If you supervise persons to whom you can pass on some jobs and responsibilities, do so. Give them jobs you don't mind doing as well as ones you don't like. Reward them for their efforts. Appreciate their contribution.

Guard Your "Volunteer" Time and Energy
Is your plate already filled with church-related activities? Say no when you are asked to take on one more committee, no matter how worthy the mission. Is your schedule already filled to the max? Say no when you are asked to volunteer your time for the community project, no matter who asks you.

Say No When Asked to Do Anything Demeaning to Your Personhood
Do you feel as if a "friend" is using you to run her errands and do her chores because she simply has failed to budget her own time and energy wisely? Politely but firmly say, "I can't help you right now." (If you lose her friendship over saying no, question whether she was really a friend in the first place.)

Childhood neighborhood bullies often seem to reemerge in the form of supervisors, spouses, colleagues, or fellow club members. There comes a time when it's best to say, "This is my neighborhood, too."

26 ★ Conduct a Language Audit

The person with low self-esteem often doesn't limit her negative thinking or negative comments to herself. She frequently becomes cynical about all of life, with a hefty side order of sarcasm and cutting criticism.

Listen to Yourself Conduct a language audit. Listen to what you say and how you say it. Use a tape recorder if you need to become more objective. Really "hear" yourself—both the words you use and the tone in which you speak them.

- Does your voice have a biting edge?
- Are you sarcastic?
- Do you project a cynical outlook on life?

Are you always suspicious of what you cannot see or do not know, always cautioning others against certain people or activities, always warning others not to take a risk?

- Do you frequently hear yourself pointing out another person's bad points?
- When you see a movie or play, read a book, or hear a performance, is your first response one of pointing out the good in it, or do you immediately zero in on what was wrong?
- Are you a complainer?
- Do you have a definition or criteria for determining when something is wonderful?

Most of us are far better at defining *awful* than we are at defining *marvelous*. It's easier for us to tell when we feel bad than when we feel good. It's easier for us to identify the missing piece, point out the error, or find the smudge on the piece of paper than it is for us to supply the missing piece, resolve the error, or clean up the mess.

Be a Truth Speaker   Choose to become a truth speaker, which means communicating the whole truth about something, both good and bad. Choose to change your tone.

Change the way you speak about other people . . . about events and performances . . . about your work and that of others . . . about life! You'll change the way you think.

27 ★ Set a Deadline

The periodic down day, the trough of your biological rhythm chart, the bad circumstance that hits out of the blue—all are a part of life. Feeling momentarily down, however, shouldn't progress into a long-term outlook of poor self-esteem.

Choose a Date Set a time when you put an end to the grieving.

Mark a moment when you choose to stop complaining about something.

Circle the date on the calendar when you are going to come out of mourning and attend the dance.

Choose a day on which you will become "available" again to date socially. If no one asks you to do something on that day, take the initiative and invite someone out to dinner or to a movie.

Move On In so doing, you are activating a decision to move on in your life—to push your boat back into the main stream of the river. You are

putting yourself in a position to laugh again . . .
try again . . . create again . . . work again.

- Say to yourself after you are fired from your
  job, "I lost that job. I failed at it. But I refuse to
  let this convince me that I will always fail. I'll
  allow myself to mourn all weekend, but on
  Monday morning, I'm going to get up and
  start beating the bushes in search of my next
  opportunity."
- Say to yourself after the divorce, "I'm going to
  give myself six months to heal and to grow.
  And then I'm going to start inviting small
  groups of people to do things with me or to
  come over to my house for potluck dinners."

Talk to Others   At times, it is helpful to talk
to another person about what you need to do to
make amends for a failure or a mistake. The idea
of penance carries over into all areas of life. Accept
and define a "punishment" for yourself, and then
once you have completed that onerous chore, that
painful process, that job, or that payment schedule
—put the mistake behind you. Don't punish yourself for the rest of your life for an error.

At times, asking forgiveness of another person
and receiving forgiveness should mark the "end"
of the issue for you. Give the quarrel or the argument a definitive end. Shake hands at the end of
the fight. Reach a decision or a conclusion after a

debate. Decide that bygones really will be bygones.

A significant portion of low self-esteem can be attributed to continuing to hang on to things long after you should have let go of them—be it cutting comments, mistakes, sins, losses, or failures. Sound a bell in your soul to put an end to the round.

28 ★ Go Anyway

The person low in self-confidence generally doesn't enjoy being alone in a crowd. He'd rather be truly alone so that he can always define his rules and choose his outs.

Have Fun Learn to go places by yourself and have fun with other people even if you don't arrive with them or leave with them. The only way to learn this is to do it.

Can't find anybody to go with you to the movie? Go by yourself. You may see someone there you know. If not, you'll at least view the movie that appeals to you.

What should you do if you're alone and a couple invite you to go to lunch with them after church? Go! Bon appétit!

Do you find yourself without a date for the club banquet only three days away? Go alone. There's so much mingling at most parties that many people may not even realize you arrived by yourself. Furthermore, once you're there, you'll find others who don't have dates, and they'll be grateful for someone to talk with. If you're bored or feel left out after you arrive, you can always leave early.

Pursue Your Interests Do you stay away from church because your family won't go with you? Go anyway.

Do you force yourself to go to the football game when you'd really rather be at the opera? Do you go to the ballet when you'd really rather stay at home and watch the tennis match? Find a way to compromise. Perhaps you can still buy season tickets to the opera for your wife and a friend, with the understanding that you're also buying a season pass to the football games for yourself and your friend's husband.

You don't need to share all of the interests of the other members in your family. You can go alone to the gallery, the museum, the shops. You can drive to the lake or hike in the mountains by yourself.

Some people fear that enjoying separate activities causes a rift in a relationship. That is rarely the case. Rifts tend to arise from other factors. Usually, two people who engage in separate activities find they have more to communicate about with each other. Both are happier doing what they enjoy doing, and their happiness rubs off on the relationship.

Guidelines In pursuing separate activities, follow some simple guidelines:

- Keep the communication lines open with your family members or those to whom you are committed in a relationship. Tell them where you are going, what you'll be doing, who you'll be going with (if anybody), and when you'll return.
- Don't exclude your spouse from the things you enjoy doing.
- Don't commit yourself to "side" relationships that might damage or destroy the family relationships to which you have already committed.

Learn to enjoy what gives you pleasure in life, even if you have nobody else to share it with at the moment. Don't blame someone else for the things you give up, or give someone else a hard time for not accompanying you to places or events to which you'd like to go.

When you learn to enjoy going places and doing things by yourself, you invariably gain self-esteem. You discover that you like going places with the person named *you!*

29 ★ Reward Yourself

Have you accomplished something worthwhile in your estimation, but nobody noticed? Have you finished a major project, but nobody applauded? Have you passed a milestone, but nobody congratulated you?

Reward yourself!

Buy yourself a present   Perhaps it is something totally frivolous or indulgent. Maybe a new set of golf clubs or a make-over at a local salon.

Go on the trip of your choice   Get away for the weekend. Escape on a cruise.

Take yourself out to dinner   Enjoy being waited on.

Send yourself flowers   This reward is especially appropriate if the unlauded success was at work. You can write yourself an enclosure card of congratulations and sign it "a fan." Keep coworkers guessing about the sender!

Take a day of vacation Spend it in whatever way you choose.

Celebrate your success There are only two rules to self-impose as you reward yourself:

1. Don't choose as a reward anything that will bring you harm or reverse the trend of your success. There's no point in rewarding yourself for a weight loss by eating a banana split. There's no good in spending a lot of money on a reward for yourself because you just got out of credit card debt.
2. Don't reward yourself in a way that causes harm to someone else. Don't be vindictive in rewarding yourself or do something to "undo" another person.

You don't need to wait for the end of a large task or long-term project to reward yourself. Sometimes interim rewards are helpful and motivating. For example, if you have embarked on a three-year course of study, reward yourself at the end of each year or each semester.

The task doesn't have to be something in the public arena. Perhaps you've had a goal for several years of cleaning out the garage. Reward yourself when the job is done!

You don't have to let anybody else know about your reward. You can savor your own sweet success all by yourself. On the other hand, you may want to invite others to celebrate with you. Let them know what you're celebrating, and invite them to come along as your guests. Be prepared to pay their way.

The goal you've reached may be in your daily routine. Do you regularly work out at a gym? Have you reached a weight goal (for your body or on a certain machine) or finally completed the number of laps you set as a goal for yourself (on the track or in the pool)? Reward yourself with an extra half hour in the sauna or whirlpool!

Celebrating your successes has two great benefits. First, the celebration underscores your success in a positive way in your own mind and memory. When you recall a celebration, you recall the success that evoked it and vice versa. You are reinforcing your own good behavior. Second, you are pointing out to others (in an unarrogant way) that you have accomplished something and that your achievement is worthy of notice.

30 ★ Learn a New Skill

Perhaps you feel as if you just aren't good at anything. Try learning a new skill.

Discipline   Learn from somebody who knows what he is doing, is good at the thing you want to learn, and is a good teacher. Learn from someone who will be patient with you as you learn, will encourage you, and yet will require you to practice and exercise discipline.

Physical Attributes   Avoid areas in which you do not have the physical attributes for success. If you have weak ankles and a bad back, you probably don't want to undertake ice-skating. You're likely to hurt yourself in a major way. If you have poor small motor skills, try learning something that requires large muscle coordination. If your hand-eye coordination is poor, don't choose a skill that requires it.

Aptitude   Try a field in which you show some aptitude. Do you really like to work puzzles? Consider computers. Many computer programs require the same logic as solving puzzles. Are you good with your hands and very patient? A wide number of handcraft items and needlework projects require only those two traits.

Interests   Choose an area in which you have a strong interest. Have you always wanted to be able to shoot a bow and arrow? Take archery! Have you always thought it would be fun to design your own clothes? Learn to sew. Do you enjoy trying new foods? Learn to be a gourmet cook, and have fun experimenting with herbs, spices, and special sauces.

New Ventures   Learning a new skill may well lead to a new job or career. The people who succeed in their careers tend to like what they're doing, have an aptitude for what they're doing, have learned their job from a pro, and are physically capable of doing the job. You can join their ranks.

Acquiring a new skill builds up both self-esteem and confidence simultaneously.

31 ★ Let Go

Sometimes we find ourselves in self-defeating, self-destructive situations or relationships in which nothing we say or do is right, communication is completely warped, and the emotional pain and strain of the relationship keep us continually at the breaking point. In such cases, the most esteem-producing thing we can do is to "let go."

Has your boss made it clear that there's absolutely no chance you'll ever be promoted or given a raise? Move on!

Has a loved one stated definitively that it's over and moved on to a new relationship? Swallow hard, cry as much as you need to, but cut the tie.

Does a person continually belittle you, ridicule you, or nag you every time you come around? Stay away.

Tell the other person you are leaving Don't just disappear or waft away or fail to show up on a Monday morning.

State your reasons for going as clearly and unemotionally as possible   If you are feeling stunted or put down, say so: "I don't sense that I have the opportunity to grow. I need to feel free to succeed." If you have been rejected or wounded, tell how you feel: "I'm in a great deal of pain, and I need to leave in order to heal." The best thing you can do for the other person ultimately is to explain what has caused you the pain that you feel or to give the reason for your leaving.

Don't be talked out of going   If you hurt enough to leave in the first place, you are in sufficient pain to need some space and time to heal before reentering the relationship. Even if the person promises to make constructive changes in his or her life, he or she will need time to make those changes.

Don't assume that you'll never be back   You may want to leave the door open for reconciliation or a return. You may want to cite specific things that must be done in order for you to remain in contact or attempt to renew your relationship. If the time comes when you know that you will not be coming back permanently, let the person know that you won't be returning.

You may not be the one who needs to do the leaving. You may need to get rid of the employee, break off the relationship with the one you've dated for a long time, or ask another person to leave your home (spouse, grown-up child, even a stay-too-long visitor or relative). If so, adapt the same suggestions: tell the other person to leave and why, don't be talked out of your decision, and leave the door open for the person's return even as you temporarily change the locks.

Spinning around at the end of an emotional cul-de-sac causes you to lose your equilibrium, and it can destroy your confidence and self-esteem. Break the pattern. Walk away. Let go, or ask the other person to walk away.

Divorced people sometimes remarry.

Fired people are sometimes rehired by the company.

Relationships can heal.

Love is a renewable resource.

Still, when a relationship has been severely damaged, time and space are necessary for true, lasting healing to occur. Give yourself an opportunity to heal and to regain your balance. Give yourself the chance for your self-esteem to be restored.

32 ★ Take a Course

Keep learning. Chart a course that promotes life-long learning. Expect to be in the process of learning something new until the day you die.

Enroll in a course of study at a local college or vocational school, your church, or a community "open university."

You may not want to hassle with credits and grades. You can nearly always audit a course, which generally means that you pay a slightly lower fee and are exempt from taking tests and writing papers but are still expected to attend classes, keep up with reading assignments, and contribute your ideas in class discussions.

Benefits   A course of study can . . .

- keep you mentally stimulated.

No matter what you're studying, or even how many times you've studied that subject before, you'll undoubtedly encounter new ideas from new people. Learning is a great "high."

- occupy time otherwise spent worrying or feeling depressed.

Engage your mind in a subject other than yourself and your problems!

- improve your communication skills.

The more you are called upon to defend an idea—verbally or in writing—the more confidence you gain in the information you know and your ability to express yourself.

- give you the needed information or skills for a new job or promotion.

Jobs and promotions tend to go to the person with the most information.

- help you become more disciplined.

In making time for reading, research, or study, you're likely to be forced to live by a tighter schedule and become more disciplined.

Accomplishment You'll have a sense of accomplishment upon completion of a course of academic study or vocational training.

33 ★ Shrug It Off

We often tease people about being Teflon coated. You know the type. No problems ever seem to stick to them as they sail smoothly through life. They never seem to be blamed for anything. That's never truly the case, of course. Everybody causes problems and has problems. The Teflon-coated analogy is a good one to use, however, when it comes to critical comments aimed at us. Sometimes we just need to let things slide off.

Disengage Yourself Is someone cursing at you because of a traffic tie-up for which you aren't responsible? Shrug it off.

Is a stranger shouting at you angrily for something he perceives you did? Do not take offense.

Is someone calling you names for no apparent reason? Refuse to be upset.

Don't let an idle angry, insulting, or derogatory comment stick to your soul or fester in your psyche.

Don't mentally rehearse the scene to yourself later.

Don't engage in an argument or hurl back insults.

You are not responsible for someone else's bad day or bad manners. Don't stand around and let someone unleash emotional steam in your direction.

Don't Take It to Heart   When someone who has lost emotional control lashes out at you in unrelated anger or frustration, don't let it ruin your day.

Don't take what the person says to heart.

Don't dwell on the words.

Don't use energy thinking up a clever quip or rebuttal.

Don't even give the words a second thought.

Don't let the person's bad day or bad self-esteem destroy how *you* feel about yourself or your day. If you do, you'll be basing your self-esteem and confidence on erroneous, incomplete information. Base your self-esteem only on what is spoken

- to you—yes, you specifically as opposed to you just because you happened to be standing nearby.
- in a calm, rational tone.
- truthfully—so that the message balances your faults against your good qualities.

34 ★ Take a Self-Defense Class

Do you feel powerless?

Do you feel scared in your own home?

Are you afraid to walk down the street by yourself?

If you live in a bad neighborhood, move! If your feelings of fear and powerlessness come from within, consider taking a self-defense class.

Learn how to prevent a crime against your person and property You can reduce your chances of becoming a victim by learning some relatively simple techniques. In a self-defense class, for example, you can learn how to carry a purse or wallet and how to dress so as to discourage the casual pickpocket. You can learn safety tips, such as walking with someone else to your car in a poorly lighted parking garage and then driving that person to his or her car.

Learn how to protect yourself if you are attacked Contact your local sheriff's office to learn where you can enroll in a self-defense class. You might also check with neighborhood organizations and community colleges.

Learn what to do to recover from an attack against your person or property Perhaps nothing is more damaging to one's sense of well-being and self-worth than to be attacked or injured. If you suffer such an experience, seek help. Don't allow the memories to overwhelm you. Don't assume that "you'll get over it" or attempt to dismiss the event as if nothing happened. Something *did* happen, and you won't be able to fool yourself into thinking otherwise; the emotions related to the experience, if unvented, will eventually explode. Get help that includes your family and spouse; you'll need their ongoing support, and in many cases, family members need assistance in handling their own feelings.

Learn how to handle verbal assaults Words do hurt, sometimes more than sticks and stones. A good self-defense course should include advice on how to handle the verbal assault as well as the physical one. If not, find a course specializing in that area.

In learning self-defense techniques you'll also gain the confidence that comes with information and rehearsal. You know what to do. You *can* handle a crisis. You *can* recover from one.

35 ★ Get Out of Debt

It's difficult to think positively about yourself if you're always dealing in negative numbers. Make a decision to get square with the world.

Map Out a Plan You may need financial counseling to help you learn how best to dig yourself out of the hole. One advisor suggests baking a credit-card cookie. He literally advises melting credit cards together and learning to live on a cash-only basis.

Put Yourself on a Timetable Set a date for paying off your personal indebtedness.

"But what about my house?" you might say. "It'll take me thirty years to pay off that one. Do I have to wait so long to improve my self-esteem?" Nah. In the first place, you might be able to refinance your house on a fifteen-year basis or add a couple of extra payments a year toward the principal, and save yourself several years and a bundle of cash in the process. Generally speaking, however, your house is an asset. It has value at tax time, and it's likely to appreciate in value.

Open a Savings Account and a Retirement Account Even as you are reducing your debts, set aside a portion of money each month to add to the assets column in your ledger. Having money in savings sends a signal to your inner self: "Not only am I worth my weight in gold, but I've got some gold that's growing in weight!"

As you pay off your bills, add more to your savings account. Branch out into investments that are secure, perhaps government-secured certificates of deposit and high-quality stocks, municipal bonds, and so forth. Again, work with an expert.

Just imagine how good you will feel when the day arrives that

- you have no debts on which interest is accruing.
- all of your possessions are clearly your own.
- the mortgage on your home is paid in full.
- you have a substantial amount of money in savings, retirement accounts, and secure investments.

36 ★ Get a Job

Feeling out of the mainstream of society? Feeling as if nobody needs you—or needs you anymore? Find a job. Give it your best effort. Enjoy all its benefits!

Good Old-Fashioned Work Nothing dissipates a feeling of worthlessness (and the self-pity accompanying it) like getting a job. The advantages to your self-esteem are numerous.

The amount of money a person earns is not a true measure of character—not even a true indicator of value in society—but it is an indicator that the person is contributing toward his own good and the good of others. A job helps *you see yourself as part of the ongoing process* of a productive community.

Even if you volunteer your time and don't bring home a paycheck, you will see obvious ways in which *you are contributing to others*. If you aren't there, the job won't get done. Filling a niche says to your inner self, "I am needed. This job wouldn't have been done if I hadn't done it."

You are accountable to others—to persons on all levels of the organizational chart. In being accountable to others, you'll have a sense of responsibility to them and for them. Again, nobody fills that slot at any one time except you.

Having a job helps *you discipline other areas of your life.* It tends to make you more conscious of your communication skills. The better you communicate in the marketplace, the more others tend to respect you. The more they show respect, the more you tend to respect yourself.

You see progress in your life. Projects are completed . . . widgets are made . . . publications are printed and circulated . . . people are helped . . . clients or customers are satisfied . . . contracts are won. Sales charts show growth. Raises and promotions are awarded for good performance. New skills are acquired in the course of doing.

In having a job, you put yourself into a position where your personal growth in skills and your accomplishments can be more readily noted and rewarded by others—and if not by others, certainly by yourself!

37 ★ Have a Make-Over

Physical appearance has a direct impact on self-esteem. We all know the feelings we've had on a day when our hair just wouldn't lie down, we were "caught" without makeup, or we showed up at what we thought was to be a casual event way underdressed. We wanted to run and hide. And those feelings probably seeped into our broader self-perception, slightly contaminating our esteem and confidence.

Looking good directly relates to feeling good about ourselves.

Nearly all of us learn how to choose clothes, comb our hair, apply makeup or shave, and accessorize from our parents. But some of our parents didn't know much.

Others of us are still stuck in the look we had twenty years ago.

The moment comes for each of us when, as adults, we should avail ourselves of a professional make-over to best determine our own look. Start from scratch. Forget what you did in the past. Visit professionals and learn the following:

How to Do Your Hair You may need to work with a stylist through several haircuts or even a few experiments with perms and color before you settle on the best look for you right now. Ask the stylist to show you some tricks and techniques you can use at home to achieve the look you want. Tell your stylist about the way you live—for example, if you travel a great deal, have nonstop days from the office to social events, or engage in lots of sporting activities. Let the stylist suggest a style appropriate for your activity level, your ability to work with your hair, your hair type, and the shape of your face. You may want to explore the world of wigs or toupees.

How to Apply Makeup Insist the person teach you several looks: daytime professional, daytime casual, nighttime glamorous, and special techniques for times when you are to be photographed.

How to Dress You may want to avail yourself of color analysis or proportional analysis. Many consultants now use computers to show you the way to achieve different looks or what you might look like in various styles. Have someone work with you who can help you pull a wardrobe together for maximum coordination and minimal expense. Learn the names of new types of garments. Ask questions of those who wait on you. Ask, "What goes with this?" "How do I wear this?"

"What do you suggest for my height and body shape?" Have your garments altered as necessary so that they always fit.

How to Accessorize Consider your eyeglasses to be your foremost accessory if you wear them. Learn how to choose items for correct proportion; watch others to see when certain types of jewelry, shoes, and purses are most appropriate. Get help in matching ties to suits and sportswear. Learn to tie scarves. Explore the world of hats.

Make fashion work for you in building up your self-esteem. Don't adopt a look just because it's the "in" thing. Adopt the look that's right for *you*. In so doing, you'll be able to face the world each day with an attitude of putting your best face forward!

38 ★ Try a New Experience

Do something you haven't done before. Try something you've always wanted to try. Explore a part of the world you've always longed to see.

Gaining new experience is a wonderful way for building up confidence that you can scout out and savor the world . . . and survive! The more successful fun experiences you have, the more you grow in a sense of self-value.

You need to follow only three guidelines in maximizing the self-esteem and confidence benefits that a new experience can afford you:

1. Choose something you *really want to do*   Don't be talked into doing something or going somewhere just because everybody else is. Chart your own course.

2. Choose an activity or a trip that you can afford in terms of both money and time   Debt and exhaustion are two experiences you can do without. (In fact, they are counterproductive to healthy esteem.)

3. Choose an activity in keeping with your moral code   Don't rebel against your value system. You'll experience guilt, and that's an experience unrelated to improved self-esteem and confidence.

If you've always wanted to learn to ballroom dance . . . sign up for the special set of free lessons now being offered.

If you've always wanted to learn to pilot a plane . . . save up your cash and take lessons.

If you've always dreamed of going to Paris . . . start mapping out a plan for getting there.

If you've always dreamed of taking a cruise ship to Alaska . . . start talking to your travel agent.

Don't assume that you'll go "someday." Someday rarely comes in time. Start setting dates and making plans. In some cases, the activity you dream of pursuing may require you to be in better physical shape than you're in today; start working out and getting ready.

New experiences build you up. They expand your horizons. They yield good material for musing, conversing, daydreaming, and remembering. They add to the substance of your thought life and build up your courage to take new risks in the future.

What's the new experience *you'd* like to try?

39 ★ Face the Scary Thing

Earlier we talked about facing your biggest fear—the feeling of being alone. The "scary thing" is not your biggest fear, but it can be a crippling fear. The scary thing is what causes panic to strike you in the pit of your stomach, your hands to go clammy, and your mouth to go dry.

Are you afraid

- of dogs?
- of flying?
- of driving?
- of spiders?
- of speaking to a group of people or even standing in front of a group of people?

Stunted Growth   Many times the fears that we acquire as children can haunt us all of our lives. Such fears stunt our growth in a certain area. When that happens, we are less confident as a whole than we can be or should be—and *without* any confidence in that one area of normal life and experience.

Conquered Fears Face up to the scary thing! Seek help in getting over it.

Work with someone who can help you overcome your phobia about dogs, birds, spiders, cats, bugs, or other creatures. You may not come to desire these animals as pets, but you can at least learn not to become hysterical when you find yourself in the same room with them!

Sign up for a "fear of flying" course. Several airlines now offer them.

Join Toastmasters. Learn to face people and speak your mind before them.

Are you scared of horses because one nibbled at you when you were seven years old? Take an equestrian class.

Are you scared to be around water because you never learned to swim? Learn to swim!

Are you scared to get back on a bicycle because you once had a terrible fall? Try again!

When you take on the scary thing and conquer it, you can't help experiencing a great burst of confidence and self-esteem. Where you were once lame, you're now able to walk. What cause for joy!

40 ★ Compliment Others

One of the best things a person with low self-esteem can do is to learn to compliment others. Very often the person of low esteem says to himself,

> *"I can't compliment others. It will take away from who I am, and I don't have anything to give away."*

Or he says,

> *"I shouldn't compliment that person. I'm a nobody, and she's a somebody who doesn't need or want my compliment."*

Both are false conclusions.

Give and Receive   The more you compliment others, the more others will find something to compliment in you. The more they return your compliment (perhaps not immediately, but eventually), the more you will feel built up on the inside.

Everybody needs compliments. We can all use one more! In complimenting another person, you have the self-satisfaction of knowing that you have given something of benefit to another person. That sends a message to your inner self, "I am capable of giving to another person without losing. The good stuff inside me is more permanent than I thought."

Proper Delivery When you compliment others, keep these things in mind:

- Be genuine.

Speak sincerely. Don't say something you don't truly believe. Avoid using extremes, such as "greatest" or "most."

- Be discreet.

Don't make your compliment a show. You might want to write a note or speak to the person after all others have left his or her side.

- Be personal in your comments.

Say, "Your sermon really meant a lot to me because it caused me to think about some things in a new way," or "I laughed all the way through your skit; I needed a laugh today. Thanks for giving me one."

• Be brief and to the point.

You can always say simply, "Congratulations," or "I'm glad you won," or "I'm happy for you," or "Way to go." Don't overstate your case, take up too much of the person's time, or gush. Make your point and move on. A compliment shouldn't turn into an embarrassing moment for you or the person.

The person who imparts a blessing is an individual of inner strength of character. Imparting a blessing helps build that character even as it reflects it.

41 ★ Take an Aptitude or Personality Profile Test

You may be suffering from a lack of confidence and self-esteem stemming in part from your failure to discover the things for which you have innate talent and at which you have a great chance for success.

Aptitude Test One way to discover your talents is to take an aptitude test.

Most career planning or counseling centers at junior colleges or colleges can help you locate an appropriate test and may even be able to administer one to you. Employment agencies sometimes offer such tests, as do many private counselors and psychologists. You might also check with a minister at your church or the staff nurse or psychologist associated with your corporation.

Different tests evaluate different aptitudes and measure them in different ways, but generally speaking, you should be able to emerge from an aptitude test knowing more about your

- mechanical ability.
- creative ability.
- reasoning ability (logic).

Many tests can point you toward careers and jobs for which you are best suited as well as tell you basic aptitude strengths and weaknesses.

Personality Profile   Other tests are available to help you discover more about the way you relate to other people or project yourself to others. Myers-Briggs is perhaps the most famous of them.

It's comforting for many people to realize in taking these tests that they aren't better or worse than other people, only different. There's no such thing as a right set of aptitudes or a right personality. You possess a unique set of inherent abilities, likes and dislikes, and propensities. You show signs of your unique personality within hours after birth.

42 ★ Give Yourself a Blessing

Have you ever thought of pronouncing a blessing on yourself?

Many times we think that the blessings on our lives must be pronounced by those in authority over us—usually those in spiritual authority. Parents. Priests. Pastors. Mentors. Teachers. Without doubt, the blessings pronounced over us by such people are invaluable. We should avail ourselves of their blessings as often as possible. In fact, we should ardently seek to receive their blessings! But we can extend those blessings or renew them on a daily basis by pronouncing or repeating a blessing over our own lives.

Bless You! Before you leave your home . . . or start your chores . . . or begin your day's work . . . or awaken the rest of the family . . . take a look at yourself in the mirror and give yourself a blessing:

- "The peace of God be always with you."
- "You in the mirror—go forth today in the name of the Lord!"

- "Go in peace to love and serve others."
- "Go out and accomplish today all that you can."
- "As you go out into the world today, go rejoicing."
- "The peace of God, which passes all understanding, keep your heart and mind in the knowledge and love of God today. May His blessing be upon you and remain with you always."
- "May you be a blessing to others today, even as you accept with thanksgiving the good things given to you."
- "Blessed you are. A blessing you must be!"
- "Walk in strength and health and power and love wherever you go today."

Giving yourself a blessing is like giving yourself a booster shot of encouragement and confidence. A blessing is a personal rallying cry for you to square your shoulders, lift your chin, and face your day with all of your inner strength mustered and focused.

43 ★ Start Giving to Others

Seek to give your time and talents to help other people.

Visit the local Veterans Administration hospital to volunteer your services to those in rehabilitation.

Visit the local children's hospital. Volunteer to play games with the young patients.

Visit the local retirement center, especially the area in which the elderly are confined to their beds.

Visit the homebound who are members of your church.

Visit the Ronald McDonald house in your city.

Visit the homeless shelter.

Give Yourself As you get involved with individuals in need, you'll discover several things about them and about yourself:

- Everybody has something to give.
- Everybody needs somebody.
- Your help makes a difference—not only in

their lives but in your feelings of self-esteem.

Sometimes the problem you perceive in others is a problem they wouldn't dream of exchanging for the one they see in you!

Concentrate on Individuals Don't volunteer to help the masses. Seek to help only one or two people. Call them by name. Get to know them. Find ways in which you can help bring out their distinct gifts and traits. Don't seek to help humanity. Seek to help a human being.

Reach Potential Don't volunteer for service out of pity. Volunteer because you truly want to help another person enjoy a better quality of life and reach more of her human potential. Consider it a by-product that you'll also be growing and reaching more of your potential. The more you give, the more you get back.

44 ★ Adopt an Older Person

We need someone older and wiser in our lives to guide us, help us and, above all, affirm us. For many of us, those older and wiser people are our parents and grandparents. For others of us, our parents may have been older but not wiser. The person with low self-esteem frequently has parents who gave faulty guidance, meager help or help of the wrong kind, and little or no affirmation.

If you do not have someone older and wiser in your life, make friends with such a person. The person need not be all that much older than you in years. The person may simply be more knowledgeable or more experienced than you are.

Seek Out Older People   Find ways to help your older friends; encourage them and spend time with them. Really get to know them. Go places together. Share experiences. Engage in lengthy life-sharing conversations. Ask their advice; draw from their wisdom. Appreciate what they have to share with you, and express your gratitude to them.

Seek Out a Mentor   Choose someone with the same interests or beliefs as yours. You may have several mentors for different areas of interest or career pursuit. Align yourself with someone who is willing to help you, makes himself available to help, and is affirming of who you are and who you can be.

Seek Out a Teacher   A mentor is someone who can guide you in making decisions and personal choices. A teacher is someone who shares information with you or teaches you a skill. If you want to learn something, find the best qualified person you can and study under him or her.

Sometimes a mentor is a teacher and vice versa —but sometimes not. Sometimes a teacher can become a mentor or a friend. Choose to be a good student, and your teacher will not only be a better teacher but a teacher of "life" beyond the subject specialty.

In having an older friend, a mentor, a teacher . . . you'll have an older person who is on your side. You'll be involved with someone who sees a bigger picture of life than you see and will affirm traits in you that no peer can recognize. You'll have someone in your life who is eager to cheer you on, prod you on, and push you to the full limits of your capability.

45 ★ Keep a Personal Journal

Keep a record of your life. Record moments of importance to you. Write of your successes. List, for your future reference, your

- dreams—about how you'd like your life to be.
- goals—what you'd like to do, see, accomplish, or produce.
- likes and dislikes.

A Daily Diary Keeping a daily diary sends a message to your inner self: "My life is important to me. What happens to me and through me is worthy of note."

Record your thoughts and feelings, not only what you do. Record dialogues of significance, writing in detail the "he says" and "she says."

Annual Reflection Consider spending a few hours at the end of each year reflecting on the previous twelve months and writing in some detail about the year's highlights. Write about relationships and encounters that have held special meaning for you, and tell why. Explore the struggles you have had, and draw some conclusions about them.

Lists   Consider keeping a log of movies you see, books you read, handcraft projects you complete, gifts you give, trips you take, cultural events you attend. Not only will you find that a handy reference in planning future gifts and projects (or in recommending good movies and books to others), but you'll have an obvious objective source to check about what has been the input into your soul. Write a brief description next to each entry, telling what you liked most about it or what it meant to you.

Make lists occasionally about things you like and don't like, problems you're facing and how you plan to solve them, and new ideas. Getting your ideas and opinions down on paper can help you focus them and develop them.

Keep your New Year's resolutions or long-range goals in a place where you can refer to them periodically—perhaps at the back of your diary or journal. Check on your progress from time to time. Set new goals as you reach old ones.

Personal Profile   Write down in your journal how you perceive yourself. List the things that you want to "be"—the traits you want to have in your life. Identify your foremost goals. Put into words what you perceive to be your purpose for being. When you are feeling down, consult your journal. Read again about the person you are and the person you aspire to be. Never forget that you *are* your goals and dreams as well as your past accomplishments.

A personal journal is *your* reference tool. Write to yourself and for yourself. You'll undoubtedly find that you enjoy reading about yourself from time to time! In that, you're developing healthy self-esteem.

46 ★ Get It Fixed or Accept It

Do you avoid smiling because your teeth are crooked or discolored?

Do you hate going out in public because you think everyone is staring at your nose?

Do you feel too fat—or too thin—to be lovable?

Do you avoid getting too close to people because you fear you will offend them in some way?

Do you feel sorry for anyone wearing glasses because you feel sorry for yourself that you do?

Do you hate the fact that you're going bald to the point you are starting to hate yourself?

Fix the problem!

Professional Assistance See your dentist, doctor, ophthalmologist, or dermatologist. You may be able to do something about that annoying physical attribute for less money and in less time than you thought. Braces may be an option. Contact lenses may be a solution. You may want to explore the possibility of dental or cosmetic surgery. You may want to talk to your doctor about hair transplants.

At the same time, do some soul-searching with a professional counselor. Explore why and how your outer appearance is affecting your inner self. Talk over the problems you perceive your physical appearance is creating for you. Reappraise your desire for personal beauty and your expectations about how much you can change your appearance. Reevaluate what you hope to achieve through changes in your appearance.

No Excuses Face the fact that you cannot change some things about yourself. You aren't likely to grow or shrink in height, for example. Change what you can change without causing yourself harm, and learn to accept what you cannot.

Don't subject yourself to unnecessary surgery. Every surgical procedure has some risks and some potential negative side effects. Seriously weigh whether you need to "cut and paste" your face or body to achieve your goal of an acceptable appearance.

Quit complaining about your physical appearance. Work on it, do what you can, and then go with it. Don't continually call attention to what you perceive to be a weakness.

Stop using your physical appearance as an excuse for not participating, not joining in, not going. Stop using your physical appearance as a justification for not succeeding or not trying.

By Any Other Name   Some people cringe every time anyone calls their name or nickname. If you are one of those people, see an attorney—or consult with a librarian—about how you can change your name legally. Have your business cards reprinted with the name you desire to have. Start signing your name to Christmas cards the way you want others to address a card to you. Send a signal to your friends that you no longer answer to a nickname. Your name is your name! Even though it was given to you by someone else, it's within your grasp to change it if you don't like it.

47 ★ Don't Let Others Bring Up the Past

Perhaps nothing is more annoying or more damaging to one's attempts at rehabilitative self-esteem than to have another person continually bring up a past failure, hurt, or loss.

Responses When you encounter a person who attempts to bring up something that you have already forgiven and would rather forget, declare,

- "I'm sorry, but I'd really rather not talk about the divorce. I'm trying to move forward in my life and take things as they are and can be, not as they were or as I might wish they were."
- "I appreciate your concern, but that's in my past now. I know God has forgiven me for that, and I've tried hard to forgive myself and every other person involved. I hope you can forgive them and me, too, and help me to put this in my past."
- "I'm trying to remember only the good times."

- "That was then. This is now. I'm really liking now a lot better."
- "I know that's a part of my history, but I'm concentrating now on creating a better future."

More Than Crises

Sometimes the people who bring up the past are attempting to do so to show you that they are your allies. They are trying to be on your side. At other times, the people simply don't know what else to talk to you about! (Many times, a divorce, death, or other major injury to self-esteem seems to be the number one topic of conversation for so long, we forget—and so do others—that we have other interests and facets to our lives.)

Accept their interest in you, and extend appreciation for their friendship. At the same time, change the subject to something that you both have shared or might share. Show your interested friends that you have more to your life than a painful incident or major crisis. In showing them, you'll reinforce the idea to yourself!

48 ★ Attempt One Major Change at a Time

Certain events in life knock us for a loop, whether we want them to or think they will. Death. Divorce. Loss of a business or job. The empty nest. The mid-life panic attack. Menopause. A move to a new city. Retirement. Marriage. A first job. A first child. Numerous are the "big events" of our lives, and they invariably involve change.

The Big Events As far as is possible, attempt only one major change in your life at a time. You'll have a much better chance to succeed at it and thereby regain your self-esteem balance and achieve confidence in the new area, group, or skill. For example, avoid starting a new job and a new marriage at the same time, or avoid getting a divorce during a mid-life crisis.

Unfortunately, following divorce or death, many people find themselves a single person, a single parent, and a sole breadwinner simultaneously and immediately. That's all the more reason for establishing a strong support group of friends from whom you can ask help. Nobody can handle that many changes at one time all alone.

On a Smaller Scale Not only should you avoid tackling more than one major change in life at a time, but you should avoid the following:

Avoid trying to change more than one bad habit at a time Try making only one major New Year's resolution at a time. Trying to change too much about yourself overnight is a setup for failure!

Avoid joining more than one new group at a time Instead, set the goal of getting to know the people in that first group at a deeper level.

Avoid attempting to achieve more than one major goal at a time Think "sequence" instead of "concurrent" as you attempt to make changes in your life.

Avoid trying to concentrate on more than one major project at a time You'll invariably find yourself thinking about one just when you should be thinking about the other.

Avoid attempting to volunteer for more than one group at a time Being committed in too many places or to too many people generally means that you will be spreading yourself too thin to be successful or to enjoy what you're doing. The key issue here is the extent of your commitments and the time each one requires. You may find that you can juggle several small time commitments.

Attempting too much at one time throws your entire system out of whack, and rather than succeed at one of your goals, you're likely to fail at all of them. That becomes a real blow to your self-esteem and confidence, just when you thought you were in the process of growth, self-improvement, or getting healthy again!

49 ★ Renew Your Vision for Your Life

You may become so caught up in the daily routine that you forget the big picture. Take time periodically to recall *why* you are doing what you are doing . . . *where* you set out to go (figuratively speaking, but in some cases, literally speaking, too) . . . and *how* you truly want to order your days and spend your hours.

Probing Questions Ask yourself two sets of questions:

> *What did I really want to do when I was a child?*
> *What did I enjoy playing the most as a child?*

Very often, the person's childhood vision for life and the childhood activities most enjoyed come very close to revealing the person's primary talents, aptitudes, and desires. For example, it's not uncommon for the little boy who desired to be a fireman to have a great aptitude for being a personnel agent or a customer relations employee who can "put out the fires" of crisis in another person's life. (A big red car is optional.)

The child who enjoyed playing with paper dolls, dressing and redressing them with different accessories, making new clothes for them, and designing environments for them often has an excellent aptitude for entering the world of fashion retailing or some area of design (fashion designing, interior decorating, graphic art, and so forth).

What do I consider to be an ideal day?

The way a person envisions a "perfect day" often reveals priorities. The ideal day is nearly always more relaxed in pace and has more human contact and satisfying communication than the present.

Stop to consider your ideal day for a moment. And then ask yourself a related question: *What do I need to change about my schedule, agenda, and the way I live in order to have more ideal days?* (Bear in mind that nobody can live an ideal life. You can, however, forge the frequent ideal day!)

Readjustment   Use these questions to begin a conversation with your spouse. If you live alone, write down some of your answers to these questions. You'll likely find yourself coming to decisions about how you can readjust your daily schedule, make alterations in your time commitments, and set new goals (which may include going back to school or entering a new area of training). At the root of your vision for your life are your priorities —those things you decide are most important to you—and your values, the system of beliefs by which you establish priorities.

Reinstituting your values and setting new priorities based on them can lead to personal growth.

50 ★ Spend Time with Children

In spending time with young children, you'll be in the roles of teacher, helper, and doer.

Free to Play If you'll allow yourself the freedom to get down on the floor and play with children (at what they want to play), you'll be in the role of a cocreator and senior playmate.

All of these roles can build up your self-esteem. It's a fabulous feeling to have a two-year-old declare, *"I like playing with you; you're fun,"* or ask, *"Can you come over again real soon?"* or report, *"I helped do this; he showed me how!"*

Free to Renew Curiosity When you enter a child's world—really get down on the child's level and explore life with him—you put yourself in a position to renew your sense of play, wonderment, curiosity. You're likely to get back in touch with feelings and ideas that have been long since buried. And all of that can be restorative therapy for your self-esteem.

Children have a great capacity for taking risks.

Let a little of their "fearless" attitude rub off on you and enhance your confidence.

At times, association with children may dredge up hurtful memories; your friendship with a child may conjure feelings of lost innocence or evoke a desire to spare the child the pain you knew. Spare the child a description of your pain. Explore those feelings on your own or with a helpful adult. Seek healing for those bad times in your childhood.

No matter what type of childhood you had, you can always approach a small child with the intention: "I want to help you have a better childhood than I had. I want to help you see more of the world, experience more joy, explore more of your own abilities and ideas, laugh more, and establish an even greater vision for who you can be than you would otherwise experience without me." In adopting that perspective as you deal with a young child, you will also be calling forth that perspective in your life. Your self-esteem and confidence will be rejuvenated.

51 ★ Vow a Better Vow

We don't have a mechanism in our culture for "undoing" a vow after it's made. Our intentions and commitments are rarely undone in a ceremonious, helpful, or hopeful manner that is equitable and beneficial to all parties involved. We *break* our promises. We *break* hearts. We *break* up families or associations. We *break* off communication. In the process, we break a part of who we are.

The only way out of a broken vow is to make a better one.

The Standard A "better vow" looks toward the future and sets a higher standard. It replaces the previous vow, not negating the value of the one broken but expressing a desire rooted in hope and determination that the future will bring healing and greater strength.

Generally speaking, make the better vow in yourself and for yourself. Don't vow to do something because someone else is insisting that you make a vow or nagging you to do so. You'll inevitably break such a vow. Make only those vows in which you require something of yourself—usually something more or something better. Then, value yourself enough to fulfill the vow you've made to yourself!

The Commitment Don't make a public declaration of commitment or intention unless you are 100 percent serious about pursuing that commitment and are determined with maximum determination that you are going to do *whatever* it takes to fulfill your new obligation—including doing things you may find painful or difficult. For example, don't vow to your child that you'll never miss another major performance in his life if you aren't willing to tell your boss no when he asks you to attend the Friday night training session.

The Positive Keep your vows positive. Don't say to yourself, "I'm never going to get another divorce." Say instead, "When I remarry, I vow to give my marriage my utmost effort and make it my highest priority relationship."

Don't make a vow that impinges upon or negates one you've already made and to which you are still committed. In other words, don't use a "new vow" to undermine one still in effect or to break an existing vow. For example, don't vow to a partner that you're going to give your best ideas and energy to a part-time enterprise if you've already made a vow within yourself to succeed at your full-time job and be the best employee your company has!

The Attainable

Finally, don't make your "better vow" lightly. Weigh your past failures. Seriously evaluate your desire and ability to make certain changes. Undertake only the vows that you realistically can expect to keep. Commit only to what you believe is attainable. For example, don't vow to yourself that you're going to do whatever it takes to become an Olympic swimmer if you're presently fifty years old!

Vows are the most serious declarations you can make to others and to yourself. Take them seriously. Do what it takes to fulfill them. When you break one, replace it with a better vow. In making and keeping vows, you'll undergird your self-esteem in a way that nothing else can.

52 ★ Ask God's Help

Turn to your Creator for a sense of your identity. He fashioned you. Trust Him to be able to

- show you a way of restoration.
- reveal to you a path of deliverance.
- heal what is sick . . . mend what is broken . . . and restore what is injured.
- help you identify areas in which you need to make changes, and give you the energy and willpower to make them.
- put back together the shattered pieces of your life.
- cleanse your memories and free you from guilt.
- show you who He created you to be.

Admit to your Creator that you are wounded . . . inadequate. Ask God to help you.

Rely on the Divine Helper There's only so much you can do to build your self-esteem and confidence. There's only so much that others can do to help you. Avail yourself of divine wisdom and strength. He who created you knows everything about you, including your full potential. Explore who you are as a human being fashioned by Him. Aim at all you can be, as He has uniquely made you.